The photo book

Story by Beverley Randell
Illustrated by Elspeth Lacey

Here is the photo book.

Mom　　　Dad　　　Kate　　　Nick

Nicola

James

Mom is in the book.

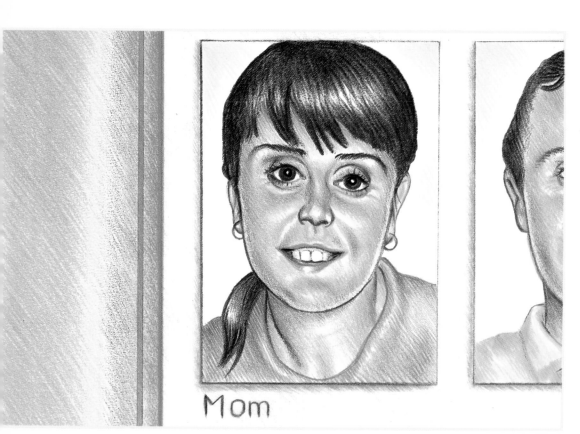

Mom

Dad is in the book.

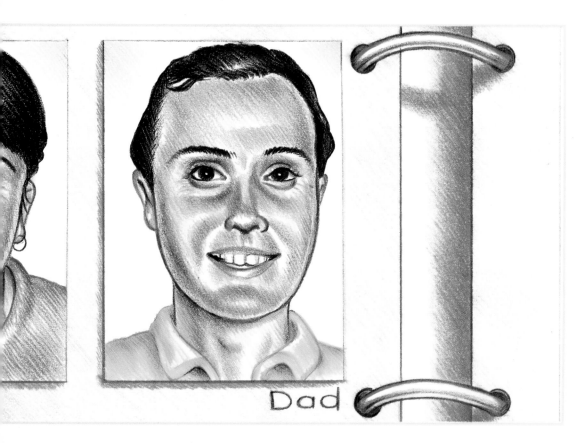

Dad

James is in the book.

Here is James.

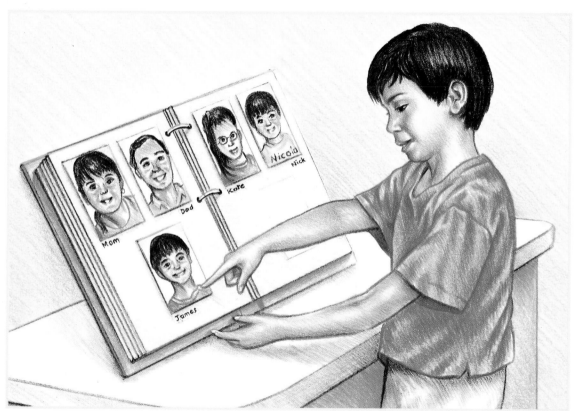

Mom

Dad

Kate

Nicola

Nick

James

Kate is in the book.
Here is Kate.

Nick is in the book.

Here is Nick.

Here is Teddy Bear.

Teddy Bear is in the book, too.

Mom Dad Kate Nicola Nick James Teddy Bear